D1274415

21st Century
Basic Skills
Library

HOW'S THE WEATHER IN SUMMER?

1

by Rebecca Felix

Cherry Lake Publishing • Ann Arbor, Michigan

Published in the United States of America
by Cherry Lake Publishing
Ann Arbor, Michigan
www.cherrylakepublishing.com

Consultant: Marla Conn, ReadAbility, Inc.
Editorial direction and book production: Red Line Editorial

Photo Credits: holbox/Shutterstock Images, cover, 1; Zurijeta/Shutterstock
Images, 4; Kushch Dmitry/Shutterstock Images, 6; Daniel Cole/Hemera/
Thinkstock, 8; Golden Pixels LLC/Shutterstock Images, 10; BMCL/
Shutterstock Images, 12; photowings/Shutterstock Images, 14; Geanina
Bechea/Shutterstock Images, 16; Lukiyanova Natalia/frenta/Shutterstock
Images, 18; Eduard Kyslynskyy/Shutterstock Images, 20

Library of Congress Cataloging-in-Publication Data
Felix, Rebecca, 1984-
  How's the weather in summer? / by Rebecca Felix.
     pages cm -- (Let's look at summer)
  Includes index.
  Audience: 006.
  Audience: K-3.
  ISBN 978-1-63137-596-5 (hardcover) -- ISBN 978-1-63137-641-2 (pbk.)
-- ISBN 978-1-63137-686-3 (pdf ebook) -- ISBN 978-1-63137-731-0 (hosted
ebook)
  1. Summer--Juvenile literature. 2. Weather--Juvenile literature. I. Title. II.
Series: Felix, Rebecca, 1984- Let's look at summer.

  QB637.6.F44 2014
  551.6--dc23
                                        2014004447

Cherry Lake Publishing would like to acknowledge the work of The
Partnership for 21st Century Skills. Please visit www.p21.org for more
information.

Printed in the United States of America
Corporate Graphics Inc.
July 2014

TABLE OF CONTENTS

Summer Is Here

Summer is here. Weather gets warmer.

6

Sun and Heat

The sun is out longer each day. This makes it hot.

Summer

North

Earth

South

Sun

The northern part of Earth **tilts** toward the sun. The sun's **rays** hit it more **directly**. This also makes it hot.

Keeping Cool

People spend more time outside. They find ways to keep cool.

What Do You See?

What kind of animal is this?

Many animals become **active**.
Some hide to keep cool.

What Do You See?

Where is the lightning?

14

Storms

There are many thunderstorms in summer.

Growing Plants

Rain from storms helps plants grow.

What Do You See?

Which fruit is this?

18

Sun and heat help, too. Many fruits **ripen**.

Soon, weather cools. What season is next?

Find Out More

BOOK

Latta, Sara L. *Why Is It Summer?* Berkeley Heights, NJ: Enslow, 2012.

WEB SITE

Seasons—Turtle Diary

www.turtlediary.com/kindergarten-games/science-games/ seasons.html

Watch a video about the weather in all four seasons and how people adapt to it.

Glossary

active (AK-tiv) busy, with a lot of energy

directly (duh-REKT-lee) straight from one point to another

rays (RAYZ) thin beams of light from the sun

ripen (RYPE-in) to become ready to eat

tilts (TILTS) leans or tips to one side

Home and School Connection

Use this list of words from the book to help your child become a better reader. Word games and writing activities can help beginning readers reinforce literacy skills.

active	heat	outside	summer
animals	helps	part	sun
become	hide	people	thunderstorms
cool	hit	plants	tilts
day	hot	rain	time
directly	keep	rays	toward
each	lightning	ripen	warmer
Earth	longer	season	ways
fruit	next	spend	weather
grow	northern	storms	

What Do You See?

What Do You See? is a feature paired with select photos in this book. It encourages young readers to interact with visual images in order to build the ability to integrate content in various media formats.

You can help your child further evaluate photos in this book with additional activities. Look at the images in the book without the What Do You See? feature. Ask your child to describe one detail in each image, such as a food, activity, or setting.

Index

About the Author

Rebecca Felix is an editor and writer from Minnesota. Winter there is very cold. But summer weather there is hot! Lots of sunshine is Rebecca's favorite thing about summer weather.